SPORTS

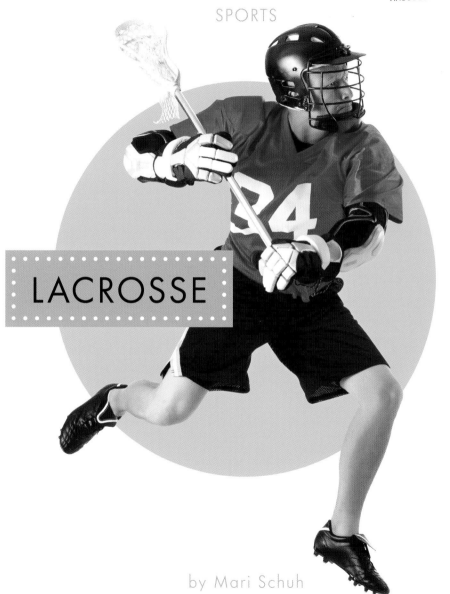

LACROSSE

by Mari Schuh

AMICUS | AMICUS INK

crosse

referee

Look for these words and pictures as you read.

ball

goal

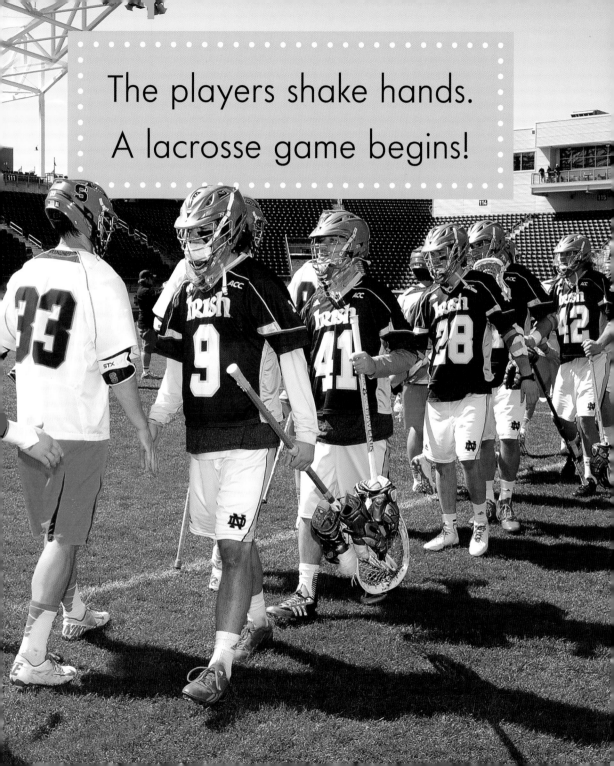

The players shake hands.
A lacrosse game begins!

The players are ready to play.
They wear headgear.
They wear mouth guards, too.

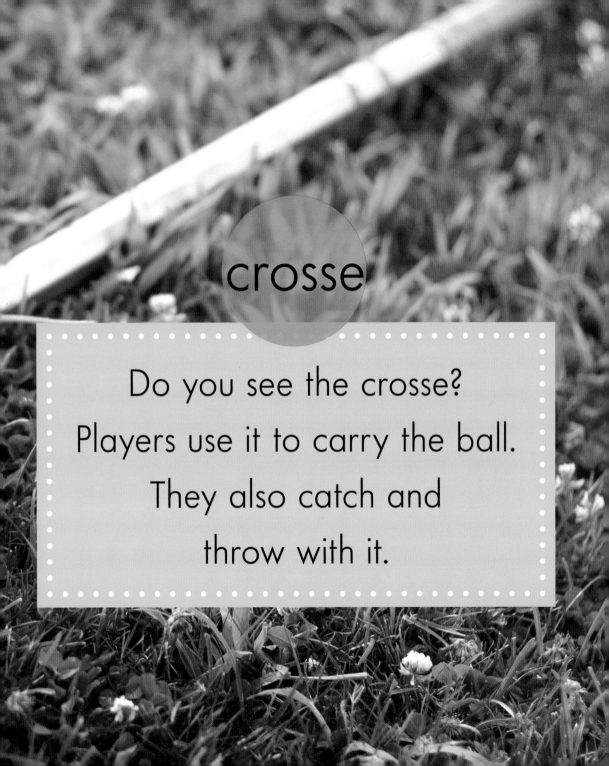

crosse

Do you see the crosse?
Players use it to carry the ball.
They also catch and
throw with it.

Do you see the ball?

It is rubber.

A player throws the ball.

ball

Do you see the referee?
He blows his whistle.
A player broke a rule.

referee

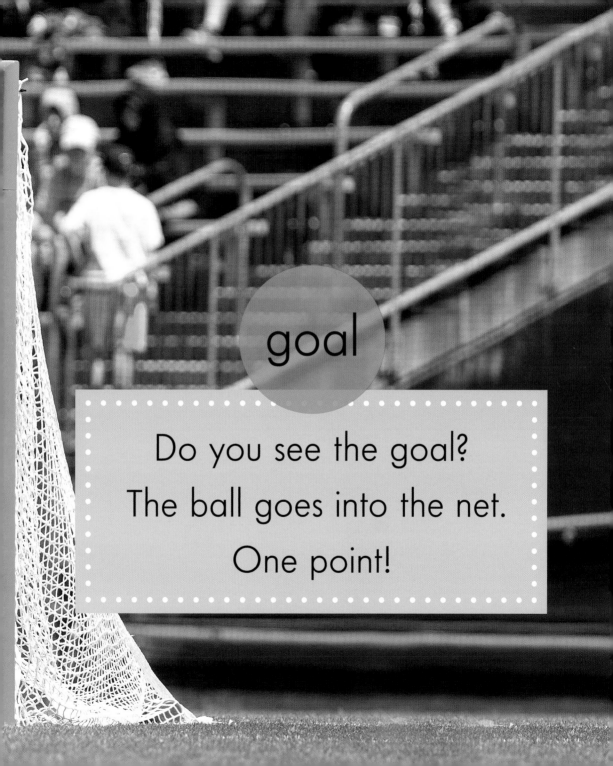

goal

Do you see the goal?
The ball goes into the net.
One point!

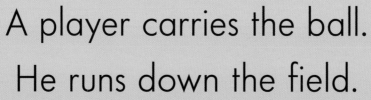

A player carries the ball.
He runs down the field.
He is fast!

crosse

referee

Did you find?

ball

goal

Spot is published by Amicus and Amicus Ink
P.O. Box 1329, Mankato, MN 56002
www.amicuspublishing.us

Library of Congress Cataloging-in-Publication Data
Names: Schuh, Mari C., 1975- author.
Title: Lacrosse / Mari C. Schuh.
Description: Mankato, Minnesota : Amicus, 2021. | Series:
 Spot. Sports | Audience: Ages 4-7 | Audience: Grades K-1 |
Summary: "Elementary sports fans will score key vocabulary
 in this high-interest leveled reader about lacrosse. Simple text
 and color photos touch on equipment, players, and rules. A
 search-and-find feature reinforces key vocabulary"-- Provided
 by publisher.
Identifiers: LCCN 2019037100 (print) | LCCN 2019037101
 (ebook) | ISBN 9781681519364 (Library Binding) | ISBN
 9781681525839 (Paperback) | ISBN 9781645490210 (PDF)
Subjects: LCSH: Lacrosse--Juvenile literature. | Illustrated
 children's books. | Readers.
Classification: LCC GV989.14 .S36 2021 (print) | LCC
 GV989.14 (ebook) | DDC 796.36/2--dc23
LC record available at https://lccn.loc.gov/2019037100
LC ebook record available at https://lccn.loc.gov/2019037101

Printed in the United States of America

HC 10 9 8 7 6 5 4 3 2 1
PB 10 9 8 7 6 5 4 3 2 1

For Natalie of Fairmont,
Minnesota —MS

Gillia Olson, editor
Deb Miner, series designer
Aubrey Harper, book designer
 and photo researcher

Photos by Alamy/RubberBall
cover, 16; AP/Anthony Nesmith
4–5, Mike Langish 14–15, Mingo
Nesmith/Icon Sportswire 12–13,
Rich Barnes 3, Winslow Townson
10–11; iStock/4x6 1, Ben Haslam
cover, Ivan Grgic 8–9, jaboardm
8–9, Paperwayte 6–7

LACROSSE